my

HINDU
FAITH

About this book

The titles in the *My Faiths* collection are designed to introduce young children to the six world faiths and each focuses on a child and his or her family from a particular faith community. While the approach and the language level are appropriate for young readers, some of the key concepts will need to be supported by sensitive clarification by an adult. The *Notes for Teachers and Parents* on pages 4 and 5 provide extra information to help develop children's knowledge and understanding of the different beliefs and traditions.

Distributed in the United States by
Cherrytree Books
1980 Lookout Drive
North Mankato, MN 56001

U.S. publication copyright © Cherrytree Books 2006
International copyright reserved in all countries. No part of this book may be reproduced in any form without written permission from the publisher.
Library of Congress Cataloging-in-Publication Data
Ganeri, Anita, 1961-
My Hindu faith / by Anita Ganeri.
p. cm. -- (My faith)
Includes index.
ISBN-13: 978-1-84234-392-0
ISBN-10: 1-84234-392-0
1. Hinduism--Juvenile literature.   I. Title. II. Series.
BL1203.G365 2006
294.5--dc22
2006040154

First Edition
9 8 7 6 5 4 3 2 1

First published in 1999 by Evans Brothers Ltd, 2A Portman Mansions, Chiltern Street London W1U 6NR United Kingdom

Copyright © Evans Brothers Limited 1999

Reading consultant: Lesley Clark, Reading and Language Information Centre
Series Consultant: Alison Seaman, The National Society's Religious Education Centre
Commissioned Photography: Bipinchandra J Mistry

Acknowledgments
The authors and publishers would like to thank Shria Suchak and her family for their help in making this book

For permission to reproduce copyright material the author and publisher gratefully acknowledge the following
Bipinchandra J Mistry: pages 7-10, 16-20, 24-25; Trip/H Rogers: top border and pages 21, 26-27

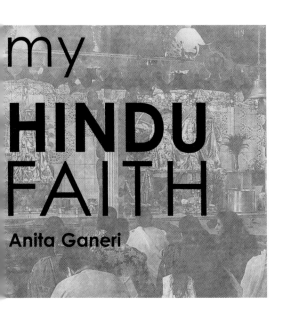

my
HINDU
FAITH

Anita Ganeri

Contents

Notes for Teachers and Parents

Pages 6/7 Hinduism is the world's oldest living religion. Although it has no fixed date of origin, its roots stretch back some 4,500 years to the time of the Indus Valley Civilization in northwest India (now in Pakistan). The religious ideas of the Indus people mixed with those of later invaders to form the basis of Hinduism as it is still practiced today. Hindus call their beliefs sanatana dharma, the eternal law or teaching.

Pages 8/9 Hindus believe in one God who is everywhere and in everything. He created the world and everything in it. This Supreme Soul is called Brahman. Brahman has many forms, which represent different aspects of his power. These forms are the thousands of gods and goddesses of Hinduism. Many Hindus chose one or more of these deities to worship. Among the most popular are the great gods, Vishnu and Shiva, and two avatars (incarnations) of Vishnu, Rama and Krishna. Ganesha is the god of wisdom and removes obstacles from "new starts" such as moving house, going on a journey, or getting married. In the mandir or home shrine, the deity's presence is represented by a sacred image, called a murti, or a picture.

Pages 10/11 The mandir, or temple, is believed to be God's home on Earth. The murtis are installed in it according to ancient rituals. They are treated as living beings, and are washed, dressed, and fed during the day. Hindus visit the mandir for darshana, or a "sight" of the deity.

Pages 12/13 The Hindu act of worship is called puja. Offerings of candy, fruit, and flowers are made, through a priest, to the deity to be blessed. Then they are shared among the worshippers. This bestows the deity's blessing on them. These offerings, which have been blessed by God, are called prashad. The priest who performs the puja in a mandir is called a pujari. After the puja, he places a red mark of blessing on the worshippers' foreheads. This is called a tilak. Hindu women wear a red dot on their foreheads to show that they are married. Priests also conduct special ceremonies, such as weddings and funerals, both in the mandir and at people's homes.

Pages 14/15 Hindus also worship at home. Most have a family shrine, which may be a room, a corner of a room, or even a simple shelf. The whole family may join in morning and evening prayers. At these times, they recite a prayer, called the Gayatri Mantra, in praise of the Sun. At the end of the puja, a tray of five lamps is circled in front of the deity. The five lamps represent the five senses to show that Hindus worship with their whole beings. The worshippers hold their hands over the flames and touch their heads and eyes to receive God's blessing. This ceremony is called arti.

Pages 16/17 Aum (sometimes written Om) is the sacred sound of Hinduism, which is recited at the beginning and end of prayers, meditation, and readings from the sacred texts. It is believed to be sound of God and of all creation, and to contain all the secrets of the universe. You often seen it written on cards, artifacts, or painted on walls. The Swastika (which means "It is well") is an ancient Hindu sign of peace and good luck. During World War II, the German Nazis used a twisted swastika as their symbol, turning it into a sign of evil, the very opposite of its Hindu meaning.

Pages 18/19 Stories are seen as a very important way of passing on religious knowledge and wisdom. The oldest texts are the Vedas, collections of hymns, prayers, and magic spells, and the Upanishads, a series of philosophical works that take the form of lessons between gurus (teachers) and their pupils. The most popular texts are the two great epic poems, the Mahabharata and the Ramayana. The Mahabharata contains one of the most important Hindu texts, the Bhagavad Gita (the Song of the Lord). The Ramayana tells the story of Rama and his wife, Sita. Stories from these texts are told through plays, dance, comic books, movies, and television shows.

Pages 20/21 There are hundreds of festivals throughout the Hindu year. Some are celebrated by most Hindus. Others are marked on a local, even village, level only. The two main festivals are Divali (in October or November) and Holi (in February or March). Divali celebrates Rama's return home after 12 years of exile. It is also a time for worshipping Lakshmi, goddess of wealth and good fortune, and is the start of the accounting year. Holi is a Spring festival that celebrates the victory of good over evil and also remembers episodes from Krishna's childhood.

Pages 22/23 The festival of Raksha Bandhan takes place in August. Sisters tie rakhis (bracelets made of cotton or silk) around their brothers' right wrists to show their love and to protect their brothers from bad luck. In return, the brothers give gifts (usually of money) and promise to look after their sisters through the coming year. The festival celebrates family bonds and unity.

Pages 24/25 Hindu weddings are usually arranged, with the bride and groom's consent. They mark the joining not only of the couple but also of their two families. Weddings can be extremely large and lavish. The religious ceremony is conducted by a priest and lasts for about three hours. The most important part comes toward the end when the groom, followed by the bride, takes seven steps around the sacred fire. With each step, they make a vow, for food, health, wealth, good fortune, children, happiness, and friendship. Red is a lucky color for wedding saris.

Pages 26/27 Many Hindus are vegetarians, although some will eat fish and chicken. They believe that every living being has a soul and should not be harmed or killed. Hindus do not eat beef because the cow, as the giver of life-sustaining milk, is sacred. Cows are also associated with Krishna, whose foster parents were cowherds. Special Indian candies are prepared for weddings, festivals, and other ceremonies. They are also sent to friends and relations.

Pages 28/29 The Hindu family is very important. From an early age, children learn to show respect for their elders, bowing to touch their feet when they meet. Within the family, everyone has a special title, depending on their relationships to each other. For example, your father's sister is your bua. Traditionally, Hindus live in extended families where several generations of one family, including children, parents, aunts, uncles, and grandparents, live together under the same roof.

AUM·BHURBHUVAHSWAH·
TATSAVITURVARENYAM
BHARGODEVASYADHIMAHI·
DHIYOYONAHPRACHODAYAT·

Hello. My name is Shria.
I am a Hindu.
A Hindu is someone who
follows the Hindu religion.

Where did the Hindu religion begin?

It began in India thousands of years ago. My grandparents and lots of my aunts, uncles, and cousins still live in India.

Hindus believe in one God who has many forms. They are called gods and goddesses.

We choose some of them to worship.

This is the god **Ganesha.**
He is a very wise god.

Where do Hindus worship?

We worship in the **mandir**, or temple. This temple is in India.

As we go in to the mandir, we ring a bell. This helps us to think clearly about God.

Who is this?

This is the **pujari.** We give him food and flowers for God. He gives us God's blessing.

The pujari puts this red mark on my forehead. It is a sign of God's blessing.

Do you pray at home?

At home, we worship in front of our shrine. It is in our living room.

We light a small lamp
called a **diva.** It helps us
to think about God.

What is this sign?

This is a very holy Hindu word.
It makes the sound, Aum.

We say Aum at the beginning and end of our prayers.

Are there any other special Hindu signs?

This sign is called a swastika.
It is an ancient Hindu sign of peace.

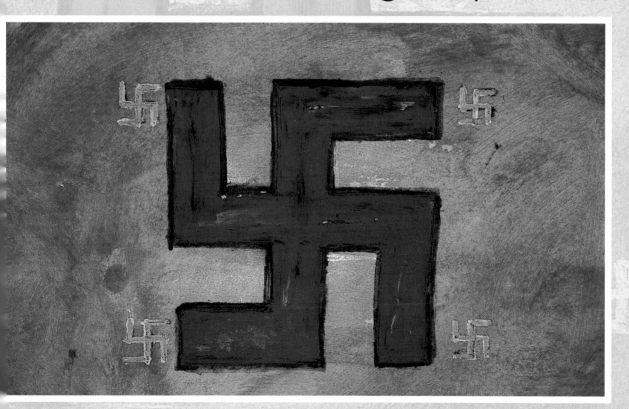

17

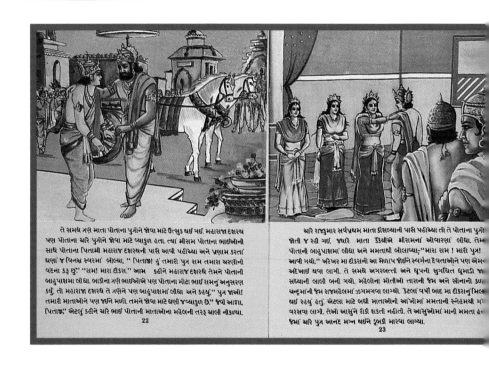

Yes, we do!
My mom tells us lots of stories about the Hindu gods and goddesses. My favorite story is about **Rama** and **Sita.**

At the festival of **Dasshera**,
we dress up and act out
the story of Rama and Sita.

What is your favorite festival?

I like **Divali** best.
We light lamps to guide Rama back
home and to welcome **Lakshmi.**
She is the goddess of good luck.

We give each other cards and presents and have new clothes to wear. At night, there is a firework display.

At the festival of **Raksha Bandhan,**
I tie a bracelet around
my brother's right wrist.
The bracelet is called a **rakhi.**

This shows that I love my brother. In return, he promises to look after me always. He also gives me a present.

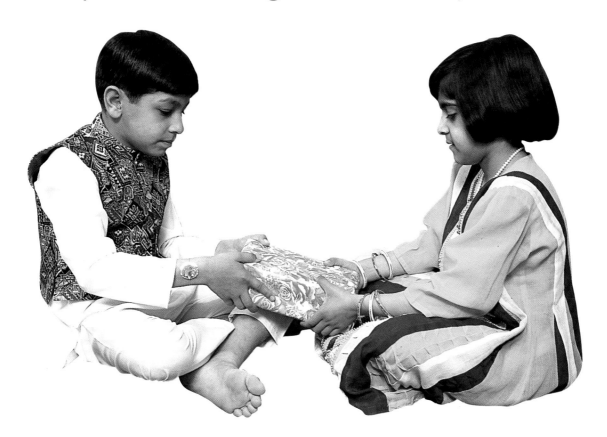

A Hindu wedding is a very happy time.

The bride wears a special red **sari.**
Red is a lucky color.
She wears lots of jewelry
and makeup.

Do you have a big party?

Yes, we do.
It's a time to meet all our friends and relatives. We have a special feast with lots of delicious food.

What do Hindus like to eat?

I like eating vegetables, rice, and bread. Most Hindus do not eat meat because we do not believe in killing animals.

I also like Indian candy.

We all help to cook and to
care for each other.
My family is the most
important thing
of all.

28

Sometimes my grandparents
come to visit from India.
We are all very happy to be together.

Glossary

Dassehra – A festival celebrating Rama's victory over an evil demon-king.

diva – A small lamp lit during Hindu worship.

Divali – A festival that celebrates Rama's homecoming. It is also the Hindu New Year.

Ganesha – The Hindu God of wisdom and "new starts." He had an elephant's head.

Lakshmi – The Hindu goddess of wealth and good luck.

mandir – A building where Hindus worship. It is also called a temple.

pujari – The priest in a mandir.

rakhi – A bracelet made of cotton or silk.

Raksha Bandhan – A festival celebrating the love between brothers and sisters.

Rama – A very popular Hindu god.

sari – A long, flowing dress worn by Hindu women.

Sita – Rama's wife.

Index

AUM BHURBHUVAHSWAH:
TATSAVITURVARE NYAM
BHARGODEVASYADHIMAHI:
DHIYOYONAHPRACHODAYAT.